contemporary furniture

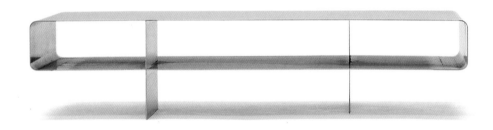

contemporary furniture

SEBASTIAN CONRAN & MARK BOND

special photography by Thomas Stewart

To our parents, who have and will always be an inspiration

contents

Compare furniture to a poem.

Poems are constructed from words just as furniture is constructed

from **details**. A wrong word will jar, producing a clumsy metre,

while a poor detail will produce **visual imbalance**. In the same

way, in our homes a wrong piece or one in the wrong place can upset

the **equilibrium** of an otherwise harmonious environment.

Y's Chair, designed by Christophe Pillet in 1995 for Cappellini. This self-skinned soft polyurethane foam seat shell set on a swivelling aluminium base is a good example of harnessing technology originally developed for other purposes. Here a process used in the manufacture of car dashboards yields a comfortable yet hard-wearing seat unit.

introduction

Where did you get that chair?

Furniture has much more to it than the primary functions of support and storage. The chair we sit on and the desk we work at have undergone a great deal of thought and consideration in the way they are made, how they work and what they look like – in short, how they are designed. It is this

A stool made from reclaimed oak and designed by Christian Liaigre proves that a simply produced basic piece of furniture can be viewed almost as a piece of sculpture.

importance of the aesthetic design that arguably makes furniture the closest that industrial design comes to fine art, often blurring the boundaries with sculpture.

From the simple austerity of the stone-age caveman to the splendour of 'Grand Manner' Louis XIV décor, mankind has been making furniture and art for function and decoration for centuries. Even in today's world – a technological global village – a remote African tribesman may well fashion a simple wooden stool that would not look out of place in the stone-age caveman's humble home. In a different environmental context, perhaps set on a pedestal in a museum of contemporary art, we might view the same stool more as an objet d'art, as a celebration of elegance in simplicity adhering to the dictum 'form follows function', rather than the unsophisticated and crude effort Louis XIV's courtiers would have undoubtedly perceived it to be.

Although usually displayed and photographed in isolation, furniture is in fact rarely seen in the flattering open space of the art gallery. Furniture is intended to be used as a component of a living space in relation to other pieces. It has to function and work visually with other items around it; relating almost in the way clothes do when one dresses either for everyday or for a particular occasion. Furniture could almost be seen as clothing for our homes, with each room having a function to fulfil. If this is so, it follows that if furniture is the clothing, then lighting and art are the accessories and jewellery.

As with clothing, the agenda for furnishing our homes is as much about our own self-expression as keeping warm and feeling comfortable. Fashions continually change and there are many

The **Wink** *chair, designed by Toshiyuki Kita for Cassina, 1976-1980, has a steel frame and textile-covered polyurethane foam. The soft rounded forms of this car seat technology-derived chaise longue are reminiscent of the works of Henry Moore.*

Egg Chair, designed by Arne Jacobsen for Fritz Hansen in 1957-1958, is a fabric-covered, foam-upholstered fibreglass seat shell on a swivelling cast aluminium base with a loose seat cushion. Even the chair's name plays on its womb-like antecedents. This chair has been futuristic for over forty years – only the base has shown signs of aesthetic age.

magazines dedicated to keeping you informed of the latest furnishing vogues and which designer is doing what. The fashion designer/stylist Ralph Lauren, for example, now influences the style of home furnishings as much as clothing. It seems that no fashion label, from Gucci to Banana Republic, now feels fully dressed without launching its own home-style collection.

There are 'classics' too, which seem to be as perennial as Chanel's 'little black dress' or Levi jeans. For instance, Charles and Ray Eames' lounge chair and ottoman (shown on page 36) and Michael Thonet's *Bentwood* chairs (shown on page 20) are forever being rediscovered by new generations of furniture-buyers. The commonality with 'classics' seems to be that they all seem to spend more time in fashion than out. The reality is that clothing and home fashions are now becoming more and more inextricably linked under the broad umbrella of fashion called 'lifestyle'.

There is however one major difference between clothing and furniture. Ask yourself how much you would expect to spend on an evening out, how much on a pair of training shoes, how much on a chair. How long will the benefit of these each last?

A good night out or a pair of the latest trainers may cost about the same as, say, a Philippe Starck dining chair. In five years, although no longer new, you may be still happy with the chair; in five months the trainers may be discarded at the back of a cupboard; in five days that night out is already becoming a distant memory. The fact is that the furniture fashions move at a slower pace and the benefits of a well-designed piece of furniture can be a pleasure and a treasure for a lifetime.

This book is not attempting to provide you with a comprehensive guide to the subject of furniture – merely a personal introduction. We have, however, tried to cover some of the basic issues and show what we believe to be some of the best new designs now available.

Incisa was designed by Vico Magistretti and Francesco Binfaré in 1992 for De Padova. It is a swivel armchair with rigid polyurethane structure covered in leather, upholstered with polyester wadding and with zippered, removable inner covering, set on a four-spoke base. This immaculate equine seat has been reinterpreted with an almost Dadaist expression worthy of Marcel Duchamp himself.

getting started

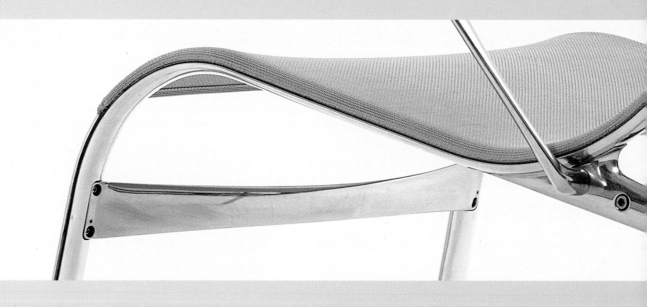

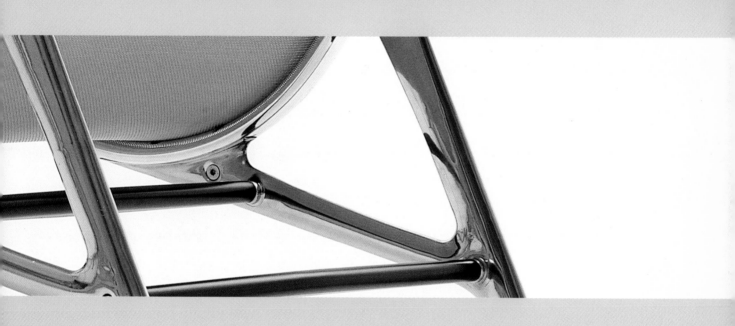

getting started

Our choice of furniture and the way we use and arrange it is what makes a house into our home.

Yet home decoration is more than satiating our inner nest-building needs; it's also another subliminal means of our self-expression – establishing our identity and reminding ourselves as well as communicating to others who we are, what we like and even which social set we subscribe to. Our homes become an inevitable extension to our identity.

Technology has also had a fundamental and permanent impact on the way we live and organize our homes. Houses were traditionally built around a very different social structure which did not encompass central heating, television and prepared meals ready for the microwave. What domestic central heating has bought us is an environment that does not require us to build fires for heat. The results of this are homes that are both cleaner and warmer; we can have fitted carpets and flexible open spaces without draughts, thereby allowing more space for larger pieces of furniture.

The way we work and the way we live are also changing, the knock-on effect of this being a change in the way we use our homes. The social landscape is in flux, and so, too, our relationship with our home environment. Contemporary furniture designers are fully aware of this tolerance of individuality and it is reflected in the spectrum of diversity of their approach. Never before in history has there been so much collective freedom to choose from so many accessible environmental styles to put together the home that feels right for us and our aspirations.

The choice of furniture and the way it is arranged can have a dramatic effect on an otherwise indifferent space. When first considering the space to be furnished, you need to decide the style that suits both your personality and that of the room. The most important practical considerations are the functional use, cost, quality and aesthetic impact on the rest of the environment, closely followed by whether it will be exposed to hordes of sticky-fingered children!

This all sounds deceptively simple, but rarely do people have the opportunity of starting completely from scratch. More often there is a nucleus of 'inherited items'

which will need careful (and sometimes brutal) editing. Decide which pieces you really love and what you will do with the things you don't (consign to the attic, auction, boot-sale, dump?). Consider your lifestyle and aspirations, and what you want the room to say. Do you want it formal or comfortable? Will you want to entertain much? How many people will use the room, and for what purpose?

Consider your lifestyle and aspirations, and what you want the room to say.

Give yourself some basic rules to follow. All furniture must have a use whether it is functional or decorative – never buy something that you cannot place, however good a bargain it may at first seem. Don't try to buy everything at once – buy one piece, place it in the room and then consider what you need to complement it. Above all, avoid clutter – a few good pieces always work better – and start with a vision.

Decide on a look that will suit the room and the building. There are many different home styles to choose from: informal, austere, original, grand, romantic. The great thing is that a different style can be used in different rooms within the same house. Don't be afraid to contrast fine, traditional details with spare, modern pieces. Think of your home as a stage.

Wood finishes and upholstered furniture will have a softer, more relaxing effect on the ambience of a room than harder, less natural materials such as glass, plastic and chrome. The choice of colour and pattern as well as the type of upholstery fabric used will also have a strong influence on the practicality as well as the appearance and identity of the furniture it's used on, allowing strong visual co-ordination with the rest of the environment.

Decoration is without doubt a very important part of the function required from furniture. Consider the underlying messages conveyed, not only to others but also to yourself, as well as the superficial issues such as adherence to fashion and appearance. Too much contemporary furniture of the same style can look a little predictable and unimaginative. This can be dealt with by introducing older, interesting pieces and art to provide a touch of history to the room.

Another major influence on the way a space and the furniture in it appear is the lighting. Too even an ambient light can look bland and dull. It is generally best to keep lights high or low – never in-between – so that the light is close to and reflects off the walls and ceiling. It is also good practice to create pools of light in room by carefully placing spotlights and down-lights so that they subtly bathe the furniture pieces in light without creating glare, but with sufficient light to work or read by.

Above all, avoid clutter – a few good pieces always work better.

Placing cylindrical up-lighters on the floor behind bulky pieces of furniture and the wall behind can produce a dramatic effect as well as increasing the apparent size of the space. Also, bear in mind that the colour and texture of the walls and ceiling have a strong effect on the light reflected off them.

The Polyprop chair, designed by Robin Day for Hille, is truly a modern classic. These daddy, mummy and baby Series E chairs are to be seen practically everywhere you look: schools, village halls, factories, offices. Available in many different forms, over 500,000 of these moulded polypropylene, steel-framed chairs have been made every year since 1962.

In the sphere of furniture, the chair should be viewed as a special case. In essence, it is no more than a simple stool with a backrest, fulfilling the most basic human need to rest. It is also an icon – the designer's equivalent of the artist's self portrait. It is now as feasible to collect contemporary chairs from different designers as it is to collect paintings, the advantage being that a well-designed chair is both beautiful *and* supremely practical.

If designers are willing to put their names to a particular product, they must be convinced that the end quality of both the design construction and the finish reflects the values of the brand that they, as leading designers, are wishing to establish. Recognized brand manufacturers such as Cassina and Vitra also play an important role because they realize that their already excellent manufacturing quality can have added value with good innovative design.

There is no doubt that some multiple retailers offer superb furnishing style at excellent prices. They are able to do this by following trends set by leading designers, expending their efforts on good sourcing and distribution. Leading designers are usually acclaimed for good reason: they produce high quality, imaginative, original, innovative and usually well thought out designs and these will always have an unmatched intrinsic value.

One thing all furniture has in common is its basic function. The differences occur in the quality of design, attention to detail, materials and manufacture. Not all designs provide the same solutions to a functional requirement. As an example, dining chairs can have different forms, materials, number of legs, finishes, back details, cost and so on, but they all tend to be made to the same height to suit the average human form.

When choosing modern furniture, always first look at the very best there is available (even if its price is out of your range) as this orientates the mind, allowing you to judge the merits of more affordable furniture. Save up for a piece you really want – it is well worth the wait and sacrifice.

What differentiates modern living from yesterday's traditions is the need to make the best use of available space, the impact of new technology and social change. A good example of this is the trend for open-plan style – the advent of the kitchen/dining/living room is due to a combination of shared labour aided by improved draught exclusion and heating methods, and the introduction of labour- and space-saving devices, such as dishwashers, refrigerators and modular construction techniques.

The need or desire to work from home has meant that the spare bedroom or a corner of the living room may now double up as a home office. The result of all this is that we need to get the maximum function out of our furniture – a sofa becomes a bed for occasional guests, daytime work equipment and papers may need to be hidden from view in the evening, a dining table doubles as a desk.

Leading designers are usually acclaimed for good reason: they produce high quality, innovative, original, practical, imaginative and usually well thought out designs.

material choices

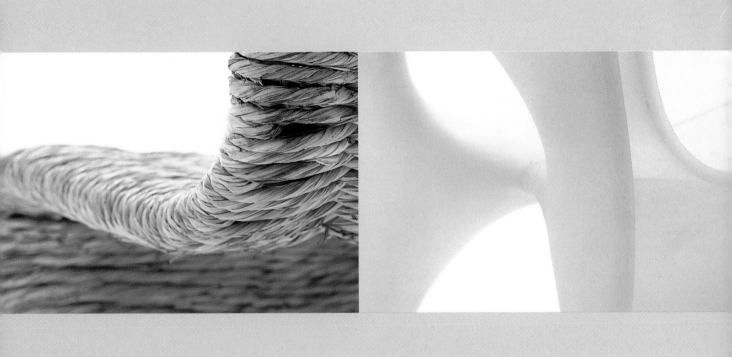

material choices

Once there was a time when rare and exotic materials were considered chic. Thankfully fashions change for the better and it is now about as acceptable to detail a table in teak from endangered rainforests as it is to trim a coat with real leopard fur.

Manufacturing methods have changed too, offering contemporary designers a previously unrivalled choice in what they are able to create and the style they can achieve. As technology improves, so do materials. Plastics for instance, once shunned as being 'cheap and nasty', have become more stable and have gained a deserved acceptability.

The materials used in contemporary furniture vary tremendously from the naturally found (such as wood, leather and textiles) to the industrially produced (such as steel, glass and plastics). The materials chosen for a piece have a profound effect on the form, style and feel of the furniture composed from them and are often the dominant characteristic in the co-ordination and theming of a living-space. Of the many considerations a designer takes into account when choosing materials and their suitability, the prime ones are their physical strength, appearance, workability and cost.

Never before has the furniture designer had so much choice of materials and industrial processes. Cross-fertilization is also at work. Complex technology created for the aerospace industry is finding its way into furniture very quickly, and the growing use of space-age technology materials, such as Kevlar, carbon fibre and composite laminates, gives strength and lightness to the pieces created. And there is always the desire by designers to make their mark by being the first to embrace the emerging technologies.

*The **Wiggle Side Chair**, designed by Frank O. Gehry in laminated, recycled cardboard for Vitra in 1972, is an interesting experiment in transferring packaging technology to furniture. The innate strength and volume of the corrugated cardboard gives this improbable structural integrity with surprising comfort.*

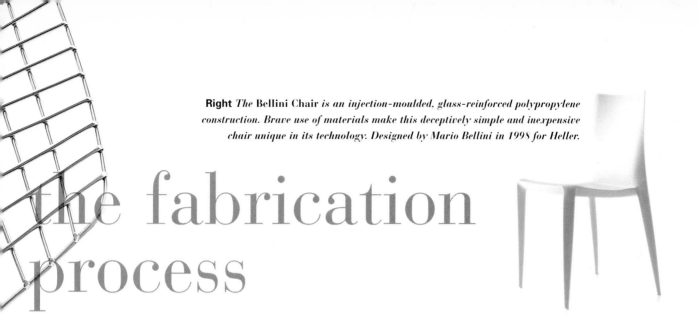

Right *The Bellini Chair is an injection-moulded, glass-reinforced polypropylene construction. Brave use of materials make this deceptively simple and inexpensive chair unique in its technology. Designed by Mario Bellini in 1998 for Heller.*

the fabrication process

The essential difference of modern furniture from that of the past is that, with few exceptions, contemporary furniture is manufactured using industrial processes whereas historically furniture was fashioned by craftsmen using traditional skills.

Industrialization of the furniture industry grew throughout the eighteenth and nineteenth centuries. In Austria in 1856 Michael Thonet was the first to use true industrial process to make furniture. He matched the demand for inexpensive, light and durable restaurant and café furniture with his new patented process based on his discovery that when heated in steam ovens, beech wood rails became flexible – almost like rubber hose – only to become rigid again when they cooled. Over 40 million of the functional but elegant *Type 14* chairs (see page 20) were manufactured between 1860 and the First World War. These were mainly used to supply the new vogue for Viennese coffee-houses.

Furniture is now manufactured using hundreds of manufacturing processes. Newly developed materials and processes such as injection-moulded engineering plastics and extruded aluminium are now commonplace.

This has had a dramatic effect on the materials used, the subsequent design options and, therefore, the appearance. Craft-based techniques commonplace in the workshop of old are now too uneconomical to be widely used.

Undreamed-of forms are now available to the designer who can construct a virtual model of his creation in the ether of a computer and view it on screen. This has the benefits of reducing the costs of repeated prototypes and improving timescale but, perhaps more importantly, it allows designer to create and visualize something that previously could only be imagined.

Even if some functional aspects have changed to incorporate modern technology requirements such as television and computers, human proportions still remain pretty similar and the basic needs of work-eat-relax-sleep remain the same.

Left American designer/sculptor Harry Bertoia's weld-mesh chair is almost transparent to light and air, causing no shadows and little impact on the space around it. Diamond Chair was designed for Knoll International in 1950-1952 and made from chrome-plated bent and welded steel rod.

wood

Wood is the traditional material for furniture. Whether it is sawn, carved, turned or laminated, wood provides furniture with natural appeal. Used judiciously, wood has the advantage of being tough, light and decorative. It is no coincidence that the fastest and one of the most successful aeroplanes of the Second World War was the plywood-constructed Mosquito, utilising Britain's furniture workshops.

The woods used today mainly come from sustainable, farmed sources where the act of growing absorbs carbon dioxide from the atmosphere, thus cleansing the air. This makes it one of the most environmentally sound materials. However, rainforest hardwoods can take hundreds of years to grow so check the provenance if in doubt. The appearance and properties of wood can vary tremendously. For example, ash and beech are both pale hardwoods that can be easily steam bent, and are suitable for structural use. They are consistent and relatively plentiful too, which can lead to industrial opportunities not available with other woods.

An example of excellent wood engineering is designer Gió Ponti's 1955 dining chair (see page 21). Its triangular ash wood frame combines the minimum of material with the maximum rigidity, hence its name: *Superleggera* (super-light). To my mind, it is still one of the lightest and most beautiful creations you can sit on.

Above and near left (top) *Frank O. Gehry's* Cross-Check Armchair *(1990-1992, for Vitra) has a bent and woven laminated wood construction. These sensuous ribbons of maple owe something to Michael Thonet's original manufacturing process.*
Far left (top) and near right (bottom) Chair 471, *designed by Christoph Zschocke in 1992 for by Gebrüder Thonet GmbH, is constructed from solid and laminated woods and demonstrates a range of different wood processes including formed laminated ply and computer-machined forms.*
Far left (bottom) *Charles and Ray Eames'* LCW (Lounge Chair Wood) *dates from 1945. The laminated ash frame and formed plywood seat provide good posture and comfort. An early classic designed for the Museum of Modern Art* Organic Design in Home Furnishings *competition, this is still produced by Vitra.*

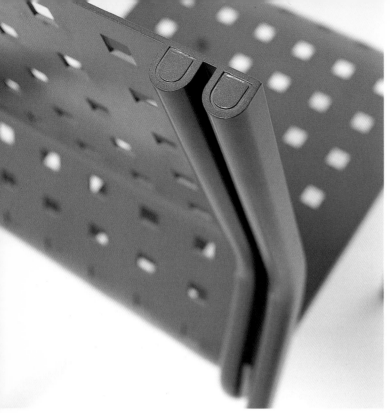

Above and below *Jasper Morrison's Thinking Man's Chair, designed in 1987 for Cappellini, is made from iron-oxide painted tubular and flat bar steel. This chair established Morrison's cerebral approach to tackling design challenges with sophisticated simplicity.*

Above and below *The Mirandolina chair was designed by Pietro Arosio for Zanotta in 1992. Its aluminium construction is ingeniously formed from a single stamping of a unique extrusion without any welding or fixings; the chair's simplicity belies the sophisticated nature of its construction.*

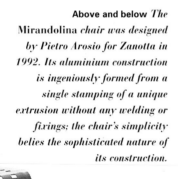

Right How High The Moon, *Shiro Kuramata's 1986 design for Vitra, is made from nickel-plated expanded metal. The springy feel of this witty take on the archetypal armchair makes it a disconcerting perch. Perhaps more 'art' than design?*
Below left Ruhs Panca *is constructed from tube and rod welded together, making this visually delicate low table-seat an interesting choice. Designed by Kris Ruhs in 1991 for Cappellini.*

metal

Metal has been used in furniture since its first discovery. Although sometimes used decoratively, more usually it was used to provide reinforcement and functional mechanisms such as straps, locks, handles and hinges. It was the invention of the wood screw that made it really useful. Early examples of metal being used visibly as a principle structure are typified by cast or wrought iron garden furniture. With the advent of industrially produced, cheap tubular steel and chrome plating in the 1920s, a new genre of tubular steel furniture arrived, typified by Marcel Breuer's *Cesa* chair of 1928 (see page 21). Metals divide into two categories – ferrous and non-ferrous – depending whether they are alloyed with iron. Like wood, all metals have their individual properties. Steel, an alloy of iron, is the mainstay of furniture; it is strong, cheap and reliable, and can be rolled into strip, tube and sheet. This can then be cut, folded, bent and welded (see *Thinking Man's Chair*, opposite). Steel does corrode voraciously so it needs to be protected by paint, powder coating or plating if it is going to be visible. Many fixings such as hinges, screws and nails are made from steel.

Bronze, a copper alloy, is one of man's oldest metals. It is quite expensive but easily cast so is usually used decoratively where its soft brown colour adds an aura of quality. Brass and zinc alloys are more affordable.

Aluminium does not corrode indoors. It is light, soft and compliant and can be easily extruded into rails, rolled into sheets and stamped (see *Mirandolina* chair, opposite), spun into dishes, machined from blocks and sand cast or die cast. It is typically used in the star bases of swivel chairs such as the *Aeron* chair (see pages 56-57). Once fearfully expensive, it is now accessible and its use increasingly widespread.

Stainless steel does not necessarily contain iron. There are many types of alloy with varying properties. Generally, they are strong and self-finishing so stainless steel can be used in thin sections. It has a hard, uncompromising appearance, but is also malleable and can be finished in many ways, such as brushing or polishing.

plastic

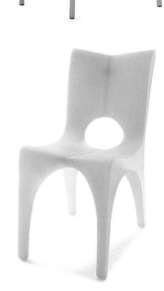

Originally developed as a substitute for horn and ivory, plastic is mankind's first truly synthetic material. As most plastics are derived from crude oil, they are often criticized for being environmentally insensitive. However, in the majority of designs this is not the case. For example, consider Robin Day's *Series E* chair (see page 18). This polypropylene chair seat might have once been a few litres of petrol or oil but as plastic it performs a useful life as a chair and can be recycled.

Although most plastics come from the same source, there are different types with varying characteristics depending on how they are formed. Fibreglass is a liquid resin reinforced with glass fibre strands and hardened in a mould. When set, it gives a permanent, hard finish on one side that can be self-coloured or painted. It is useful in furniture as it is relatively cheap to mould and size is not a barrier. However, it is expensive as it involves skilled labour-intensive work, is rather inconsistent, fragile and generally only has one good surface.

Thermoplastics like wax are heat-formable and can be moulded in a variety of ways. Most common are vacuum-forming, rotational moulding (see opposite) and injection moulding. Injection moulding, a process where liquid plastic is injected into a hard steel mould under high pressure, gives a good finish, but the making of large moulds can be prohibitively expensive.

Top right Cheap Chic, *designed by Philippe Starck for Xo in 1997, has an injection-moulded plastic seat and back and a welded steel tubular frame. Extremely comfortable, practical, inexpensive and (for Starck) uncharacteristically restrained – another winner.*

Left and centre right Chasm *is a rotational-moulded polyethylene chair. This is an innovative solution for economic small batch production runs. Designed by Will White and Katarina Barac at One Foot Taller in 1998 for Nicehouse Limited.*

Bottom right RCP2 Plastic Chair *shows an intriguing use of recycled plastic packaging. Designed in 1992 by Jane Atfield for Made of Waste.*

Above left *The* Butterfly Chair, *which dates from 1938, comprises slung canvas on mild steel rod frame. Pictured is a contemporary interpretation of the classic chair designed by Jorge Ferrari-Hardoy, Juan Kurchan and Antonio Bonet.*

Above *Nigel Coates' chair from* The Slipper Collection 60a *for Hitch-Mylius in 1995 has a beech and pre-formed plywood frame with an upholstered seat. Restrained and elegant, this classic chair quietly fits in with many different decorative styles.*

Left *The* 21 Hotel Grand Suite *chair could not be more different from the piece shown above. Its striking colours and jarring forms create charismatic sculptural forms that will dominate most surroundings. Designed by Javier Mariscal in 1997 for Moroso.*

fabric & upholstery

Wood, plastic and metal can have hard, cold finishes, be uncomfortable to sit on for long periods and can give a visually stern appearance. Textiles are easily coloured, printed or woven and can soften the appearance of an otherwise severe structure, adding texture and colour as well as being soft to the touch. Seating intended for relaxation, such as sofas and armchairs, is an obvious candidate for upholstery to cushion and warm the body.

The fabrics most commonly used are wool, linen and cotton. Wool can be dyed any colour, have a variety of woven textures and patterns, and is fairly stain-resistant and hard-wearing. Cotton is less expensive and can have woven texture, but its best feature is that it is easy to print. However, it is less hard-wearing and stain-resistant (unless treated with a protective finish).

Synthetic textiles and blends are being developed with excellent performance and new characteristics such as stretchability, which allows fewer seams on rounded forms. The techniques of using them are also changing, influenced by mass production methods. A good example is the *Wink* chair, which can adjust its back-to-seat angle and unfold into reclining lounger (see page 9).

Above *Martin Ryan's Lulu chair, 1997, is available in two sizes. This supremely comfortable dining chair supports the back particularly well.*

Charles and Ray Eames' Lounge
Chair and Ottoman, *designed in*
1956, is an enduring classic. It is
one of the most comfortable
chairs ever designed, setting new
standards of manufacturing
technology which are still relevant
today. The leather-covered
cushions sit on rosewood-faced
moulded plywood seat shells set on
a cast aluminium base.

leather

Left *Mario Bellini's Cab Chair has a steel frame with a zip-fastening, heavy-duty stitched leather covering with integral polyurethane seat cushion. The natural finishing on the bridle leather ensures that this will improve gracefully with age. Designed for Cassina in 1976.*

Alongside wood, leather is one of the oldest materials used by man, although today's soft and colourful leathers scarcely resemble the simple stuff of our early forebears, which was similar to that still made by today's Eskimos who chew animal skins to make them supple.

The laborious and elaborate processes of turning a relatively worthless animal skin into luxurious leather makes it an expensive option for upholstery. There are many types of leather, the best being cattle or horse hide. Pigskin and sheepskin nappa are also viable alternatives but less popular due to their smaller size and decreased durability. There are a wide number of finishes, coatings and embossed textures available, the finest for upholstery being vat-dyed aniline hide. For more structural uses, such as sling seats, bridle leather can look good, especially if saddle-stitched.

Leather does have almost romantic qualities that no other material can offer – even its lingering fragrance is evocative of the quality of bygone eras. Like wood, it can look even better when aged and battered. It is also very practical – only the un-coated beautiful aniline leathers stain.

Below *The* Balzac Armchair and Ottoman *was designed by Matthew Hilton for SCP in 1991. This clubby, comfortable chair, with a leather-covered polyurethane foam-upholstered wood frame with American oak legs, works well in many different situations.*

out of the ordinary

This Inflatable Chair has welded inflatable sections with chrome plated steel tube and wood frame. Space age and futuristic-looking, Nick Crosbie's chair was designed for Inflate in 1997.

Designers are always exploring new ways of making furniture, often using materials and technologies from other industries. These pieces tend to emanate from small studios where designers take risks large manufacturers cannot consider. This conceptual approach can lead to provocative pieces which take on iconagraphic status. The uncompromising disposition of their designs often means they are unsuitable for volume production and are made as one-offs or in small batches. This can make them collectable, being used as semi-functional sculpture to give an interesting edge to a room. Opting for innovative furniture may seem a risk compared to buying reproductions of classics, but it is worth buying originals. Arne Jacobsen's *Ant* chair was innovative and influential in the 1960s and an original is now worth a skip-load of the lesser quality designs inspired by it. It is likely this will apply to contemporary rising stars.

Ghost is made from moulded, toughened glass — an ingenious one-piece form that is stronger than you might think. This is similar to wire mesh furniture in that it casts no shadow and makes little visual impact on space. Designed by Cino Boeri and Tomu Katayanagi for Fiam in 1987.

King Tubby is an intriguing reinterpretation of the traditional wickerwork arm chair. Designed by Platt and Young for Driade in 1997.

Left *Tom Dixon's S Chair, designed for Cappellini in 1988, is not the most comfortable of chairs, but one of the most striking – a visually strong sculptural statement in any space.*

furniture

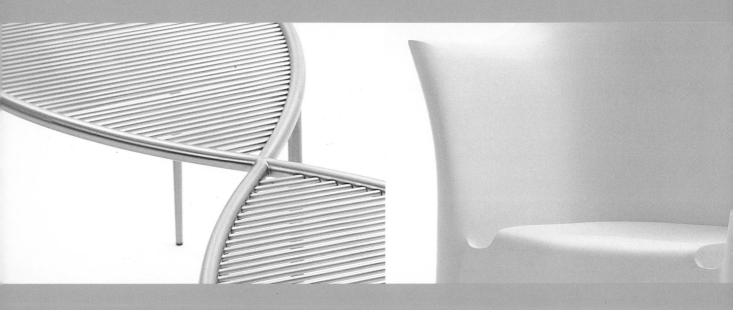

room by room

furniture room by room

This chapter leads you through the home room-by-room, showing you what we consider to be some of the best new designs in furniture, explaining how to get the most from the pieces you choose and giving some indications of current and future trends.

In our selection of furniture, we emphasize strongly the importance of supporting the talent of original furniture designers, rather than buying pallid, mass-produced imitations of their work. We believe many of the items featured on the following pages are destined to become the classics of the future, and some furniture buyers with foresight are already beginning to accumulate pieces by these young designers, believing they are the collectibles of tomorrow.

Many of the pieces we like most are the physical manifestations of an idea or concept and, as such, have a story to tell. We ask ourselves whether the designers or manufacturers were the first to use such a construction method, is the piece a homage to another designer or artist, is its form notable. As an object without heritage clearly cannot exist, it follows that the richer the history, the more interesting the piece. With art, the smaller the edition the more valuable the print; with furniture, a one-off prototype will rarely have the refined finesse or provenance of the limited edition, but ubiquity has an inverse relationship to value.

Marc Newson's Bucky, 1997, is made from moulded polyethylene and is clearly inspired by the architectural guru Buckminster Fuller's geodesic dome. This chair is based on one of the dome's modules and theoretically, if attached to enough other seats, would form a large sphere.

kitchens

The impact of pre-prepared foods, cleaner cooking technologies and improved air extraction has allowed the kitchen to become a more accommodating environment. This, combined with ever-changing social trends, has helped the kitchen fast become the new focus of the home, with the move towards less formality and the tendency for the open-plan combination with the dining room creating a larger, more friendly living space. The kitchen is no longer a hidden room but the centre for family life and informal socializing.

Out of this change comes the need to combine the functions of the food preparation surface with informal eating and entertaining. The higher worksurface required for good posture while standing and cooking is met by the introduction of tall stools for comfortable seating. Surfaces and finishes come under greater attack in the heat of the kitchen than anywhere else in the home, so durability, scratch endurance, and water and stain resistance are important practical considerations when selecting furniture in this area.

The Atlas Stool, designed by Jasper Morrison for Alais, has a powder-coated steel frame with fabric- or leather-covered polyurethane seats. The swagged bottle neck detail on the seat stem is typical of Morrison's understated attitude.

*The bar-height **Beatnik High Table**, designed by Jonas Lindvall in 1996, with accompanying solid birch, clear laquered stools works well for food preparation as well as for eating — ideal for the kitchen or the creative workspace.*

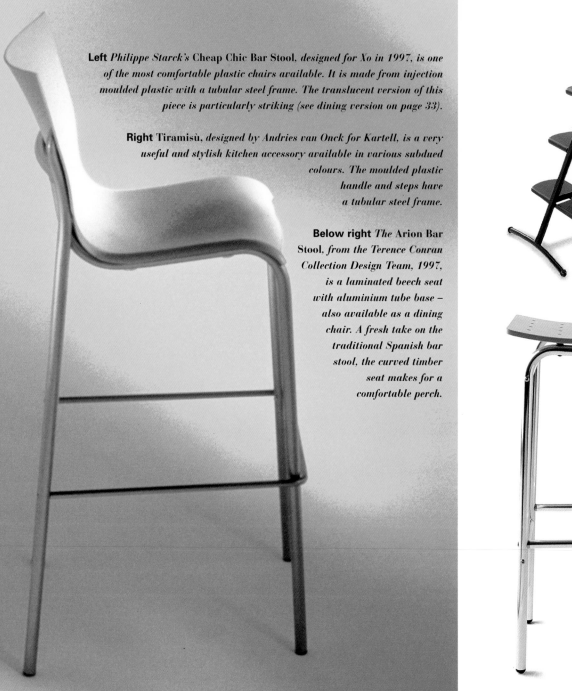

Left *Philippe Starck's* Cheap Chic Bar Stool, *designed for Xo in 1997, is one of the most comfortable plastic chairs available. It is made from injection moulded plastic with a tubular steel frame. The translucent version of this piece is particularly striking (see dining version on page 33).*

Right Tiramisù, *designed by Andries van Onck for Kartell, is a very useful and stylish kitchen accessory available in various subdued colours. The moulded plastic handle and steps have a tubular steel frame.*

Below right *The* Arion Bar Stool, *from the Terence Conran Collection Design Team, 1997, is a laminated beech seat with aluminium tube base – also available as a dining chair. A fresh take on the traditional Spanish bar stool, the curved timber seat makes for a comfortable perch.*

With modern urban life, space is at a premium and the kitchen is no exception. There is a need to maximize whatever space is available, such as with ceiling-height cupboards and shelves. To access these easily there are a variety of ingenious solutions, such as light-weight compact folding steps and more rigid combination stools. Backless stools, although providing less support, can be usefully stored under work/eating surfaces. High trolleys have many uses, not only as movable storage for large cumbersome objects like serving bowls but also to provide an extra surface for food preparation, serving and even washing-up overload.

As we are now spending more time in the kitchen environment, so the aesthetic design of the essential cooking accessories and other details becomes more evident and more important. Generous cupboard storage is essential for an uncluttered appearance. This is especially important if you do not have the luxury of fully co-ordinated cooking equipment – but beware that they don't become a repository for mismatching crockery, junk and never-to-be-used-in-this-lifetime gadgets! The dictum 'less is more' applies to the kitchen as much as anywhere in the home.

Above right Dolly, *designed by Timothy Gadd for Wireworks in 1998, has a powder-coated metal-rod frame, laminated plywood shelves and industrial castors. Useful for small-scale food preparation overflow and storing the odd wok.*

Right *Extend your reach with this practical and elegant fold-away step-stool. Rob Whyte's* Step Stool *for Aero, 1985, has a silver epoxy coated steel, tube and bar construction.*

dining
tables

By tradition, the dining table has been the daily social meeting place for family and friends. Talking over a good meal can be one of life's greatest pleasures. These days it is rare to find a dining table that is used exclusively for the purpose of dining – more often than not eating has to fight for precedence over newspapers, magazines, homework and food preparation.

Consideration of these other functions is as important as style and size when choosing. As a rough guide, a table 900 x 1800 mm (35 x 70 in) should comfortably seat six people, or eight at a squeeze. Dining table legs tend to pose a pretty similar issue - it is worth thinking about human leg space too, especially if you are going to be seating eight regularly.

Antonio Citterio's Angiolo, designed for B&B Italia in 1996, has a metal frame with timber top. Also available with an utterly beautiful glass box top.

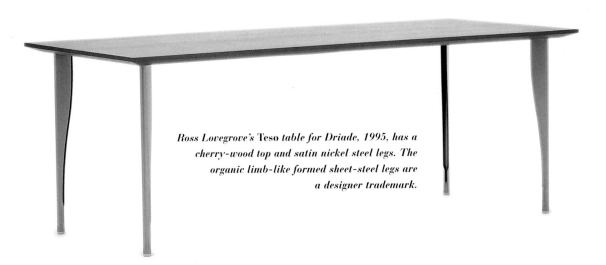

Ross Lovegrove's Teso table for Driade, 1995, has a cherry-wood top and satin nickel steel legs. The organic limb-like formed sheet-steel legs are a designer trademark.

Some people consider natural wood is the most pleasant surface to eat off. Durability of finish and heat- and stain-resistance are important too, and these are well catered for by the many types of laminates now available. Glass surfaces can look stylish, but their transparency can be a little awkward for modest diners. Rectangular tables tend to be the most practical and the best value. Round and oval tables look good – they are

Powwow, designed by co-author Mark Bond in 1998 for Bond Projects UK Ltd, has a toughened, frosted glass top set on a flat-pack steel-aluminium frame with matt silver finish. Subtlety and understatement were the objectives when designing this piece.

Simon Pengelly's 'V' Table, 1994, has a beech and laminate top. The jointing detailing is a particularly satisfying detail on this practical trestle-like table.

also easier to converse around and less cumbersome in a room, although they can be difficult to lay, especially the smaller ovals. Do ensure that they are stable, particularly if they have a pedestal base which provides good leg space but less rigidity. Expanding tables with pull-out and hinged leaves can be very useful and are particularly worth consideration if the room has space constraints and you expect to be especially social.

Daytona has folding tubular metal legs with formed laminate top with a curved lip. Designed by Wiebe Boonstra, Martijn Hoogend and Marc van Nederpel for Dumoffice in 1997/98, it is especially useful for small spaces.

Cam El Eon, *designed by Philippe Starck for Driade in 1999, has a moulded plastic seat shell with metal frame and legs. Beauty and comfort are combined in this masterful piece of design.*

Top right *Robin Day's* Polo M5 *for Hille – the polypropylene chair with the holes in it!. Advanced for its day, good value and still chic after over 30 years in production.*
Middle right Dakota, *by Paolo Rizzatto for Cassina, 1995, is futuristically styled in the millennial manner.*
Bottom right *Rob Whyte's 1989* Flower Chair *for Aero, made in silver epoxy-covered steel, is visually severe but unobtrusive.*

dining chairs

Above Dolly, *by Antonio Citterio for Kartell, 1998, has a folding structure. Sophisticated with a gazelle-like elegance.*
Below Maui, *by the 'maestro' Vico Magistretti for Kartell, is a vertically stacking chair, plastic moulded seat and back on a chrome frame. Comfortable, accessible and extremely beautiful.*

Experience shows that dining chairs can take quite a battering, especially in a family environment. People do lean back, especially when relaxed, and exert quite a force on the rear legs and frame. If this is likely, look for durability as well as style. Some of the more recent chair designs featuring injection-moulded plastic seats and metal tube legs by Vico Magistretti and Philippe Starck are particularly practical as they are tough, can be stacked and are suitable for summer outdoor use too.

Chairs with arms, or carvers as they are known, work well at the head of a rectangular table. They can be awkward and cumbersome if the arms cannot slide below the table surface so it's wise to check dimensions of both the table and the chairs before buying. It is not strictly necessary that all your dining chairs match – in fact it can be quite effective to have your six favourite designers represented around the table. It is, however, important that whatever effect you wish to achieve, it should look deliberate rather than happenstantial. It is also quite useful to consider buying eight chairs even if you only intend to set six around the table. The two spares can usually find useful homes in spare rooms.

Right *Jasper Morrison's Ply Chair, for Vitra in 1989, has a plywood section with birch-faced veneer and is available with either an open or closed back. Despite its simplicity it is strong and comfortable.*

Left *Charles and Ray Eames' classic LCW (Lounge Chair Wood), made in 1945 for Vitra. The laminated ash seat and back rest on rubber mounts which allow flexibility, making this design typically comfortable.*

Opposite below *Verner Panton's* **Panton Chair,** *made for Vitra in 1959-60, has a mono-component construction. Originally manufactured from fibreglass, it is now also available in less expensive moulded polypropylene.*

Right Fantastic Plastic Elastic, *designed by Ron Arad for Kartell in 1999, is inventively fashioned from aluminium extrusions and sheet plastic. The back and seat provides improbable structural stability.*

home office

Aeron, designed by Donald Chadwick and William Stumpf for Herman Miller in 1992, comes in three sizes, has a recycled aluminium and fibreglass-reinforced polyester frame and base with polyester mesh seat. This is our seat of choice – I am sitting on one as I write – admittedly eye-wateringly expensive and worth every penny.

As life becomes more complex and computers and digital communications continue to influence the way we work and live, there is an increasing need to work from home.

The most important piece of furniture in any office is the work chair. An ergonomically correct, swivelling chair with an adjustable seat height is essential if you are to be working for any length of time at a computer. For health, it is also very important to have the screen set at eye level, the keyboard placed at elbow height, your spine straight and your feet firmly supported.

A well-designed work chair is a pleasure to use. By assisting correct posture, it aids concentration and prevents fatigue and back pain. Try many chairs and sit on them for a while to see if they suit you. I guarantee that a good work chair is a sound investment you will never regret.

Left *James Irvine's* **Archiver** *bookcase for SCP is constructed from laminated MDF and is set on a particularly useful swivel base.*
Below *Mobil, designed by Antonio Citterio and Oliver Low for Kartell, has injection moulded plastic drawers in strong translucent colours and a chromium plated framework. It is available in several different styles.*

There are a number of well-designed home work-stations now on the market. However stylish they are, they do tend to get a bit lost amid the morass of cables and dull grey boxes. When choosing a desk or a work-station, consider future as well as current equipment requirements. You will need plenty of storage – they may talk of the paperless office but experience seems to suggest quite the opposite! Again, for posture it is important to get an adjustable height worksurface or sliding keyboard shelf. It's useful to have a means of adjusting the computer screen to be level with your eyes. A work-station with castors means you can swing it out if you need to get to the back of the equipment.

Below left Monica Armani's *Project 1* *table is made from steel with a veneered birch drawer unit. This system incorporates many different functions as well as materials and finishes. The ingenious details are subtle and sophisticated.*
Below right Bisley's *ubiquitous filing system unit is available in interesting colours and finishes, making it more domestically suitable.*

Above *The* Meda Chair, *by Alberto Meda for Vitra, 1997, is a swivel chair on five-star base with castors, with or without armrests. Quieter in appearance than the Aeron on the previous page, this chair nonetheless offers a lot of the excellent features in a less macho package.*

Right *Arne Jacobsen's* Series 7 Model No. 3217, *designed for Fritz Hansen in 1955, is a moulded plywood seat with a seat pad, set on a height-adjustable chromed tubular steel frame with double-wheel castors. Although a classic in its looks, this chair does not have the benefit of the last 40 years of ergonomic technological progress.*

Above *The* Juli Chair *by Werner Aisslinger for Cappellini, 1996, is a self-upholstered foam seat shell on a height-adjustable five-star base with castors. More domestic-looking than most office-use designed furniture.*

sofas

A large, comfortable sofa is a wonderful thing to come home to, to snuggle up on in front of a romantic movie, even when strewn with the Sunday papers on a balmy afternoon. It can also make a useful yet conveniently not-too-comfortable spare bed when that distant relative comes to stay!

For more formal social interaction, two smaller sofas separated by a low table are often better than one large one. If you have a beautiful rug or an elegant wooden floor, a higher sofa set on legs allows light to filter through effectively – it's also more practical for cleaning underneath and for crawling children too.

Sofas can dominate an environment both physically and visually so the choice of design and fabric have to be well considered, taking into account planned room circulation and aesthetic ambience.

The most important question to ask when choosing a sofa is 'Can I get it into the room?'. It is amazing how much large furniture is squeezed through front doors, only to be shipwrecked on the first landing. Frustrating, expensive... in short, heart-breaking. You can often benefit from the results of other's compulsiveness in seasonal sales, but you will have to live with their choice of upholstery. So it is wise to check whether a sofa can be disassembled and go shopping with a measured room plan, including door and window sizes.

*The **Stafford Sofa** has a moulded glass-reinforced plastic shell inlaid with foam and topped with removable covers, and American oak legs. Andrew Stafford's 1998 sofa for SCP is practical and comfortable (in an upright-sort-of-way). An innovative mix of materials gives a light, airy look.*

Opposite above Jasper Morrison's Sofa for SCP, 1988, is classically styled with subtle details. This tall piece is more comfortable than the austere lines betray. It has a beech frame with multi-density foam, feather cushion and aluminium feet.

Opposite below The Woodgate Modular Sofa System provides a very practical seating solution, if a little severe and low looking. Designed by Terence Woodgate for SCP in 1997, it has a beech frame with feather or foam cushions and stainless steel legs. The matching table completes the corner of the rectangle or square in a pleasing manner.

Matthew Hilton's Balzac sofa for SCP, 1991, has a beech frame with multi-density foam, feather cushions and American oak legs. Visually opulent in the traditional manner. (See page 37 for matching armchair and foot stool – an ideal take on the three-piece suite.)

A large, comfortable sofa is a
wonderful thing to come home to.

George Nelson's Coconut chair, *designed in 1955, has a seat of reinforced white fibreglass plastic, chromed steel base and one-piece leather upholstery. This looks like a design of tomorrow rather than one of more than 40 years ago. Although relatively obscure for some time, George Nelson is proving to be quite an inspiration to some leading contemporary designers.*

Below *Gijs Papvoine's* Olivier *is a large swivel leather chair with matching footstool which will cast an opulent aura over the simplest of surroundings – Thunderbirds' style futurism, designed for Montis in 1996.*

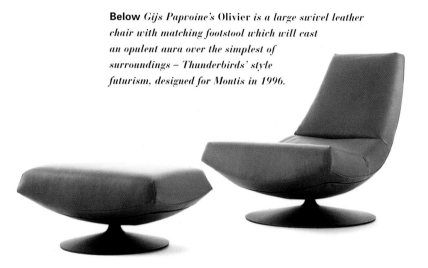

easy chairs

Apair of comfortable easy chairs can often work more effectively in a room than a two-seater sofa which modest types might not want to share. Separate chairs also have the distinct benefit of being much easier to arrange and rearrange later if you need functional flexibility in your room. The chairs featured on these pages would work well individually in most room settings, whatever their style.

A comfortable, swivelling and reclining chair positioned with good light or by a window with an ottoman footstool provides one of the best ways to enjoy a quiet afternoon with a good book.

Far left Y's Chair, *by Christophe Pillet for Cappellini in 1995, is a polyurethane foam seat shell on swivelling cast aluminium base. Soft to touch and very simple, this chair epitomizes contemporary furniture attitudes.*

Left *The compact and extremely comfortable* Swan Chair *was designed by Arne Jacobsen for Fritz Hansen in 1957-1958. It is a fabric-covered, foam-upholstered moulded fibreglass seat shell on a swivelling cast aluminium base. Designed by a master, its classic looks are as relevant today as they ever were.*

If there is the space around them, large lounge chairs and chaise-longue recliners can be a good opportunity to make a strong visual statement setting the scene for the rest of the environment. This is especially so if they are as dramatic and sculptural as are these classic pieces created by Charles Eames and Arne Jacobsen. Although both are well over 40 years old, these designs still have a powerfully contemporary aesthetic which is only betrayed by their period bases. A lounger can also be a favourite friend that welcomes you home with a relaxing recline after a long day or a tiring journey.

Right *The Egg Chair, by Arne Jacobsen for Fritz Hansen, 1957-1958, is a definitive icon of 1950s' furniture design. It is a popular prop in many movies, from James Bond to 2001 Space Odyssey. It has a fabric-covered, foam-upholstered moulded fibreglass seat shell on a swivelling cast aluminium base with loose seat cushion.*

Above La Chaise *by Charles and Ray Eames is a fibreglass seat shell on a wood and rod base. Although not originally put into production, this amoebic-shaped chair seems to be inspired by the work of the then contemporary sculptor Henry Moore. Without moving parts, the form gives a choice of several positions from recline to upright. Designed in 1948, it is now made by Vitra.*

other seating

When shopping for furniture for relaxing, don't limit yourself to sofas and easy chairs – there's a good choice of alternatives now available from leading designers. Super-sized floor cushions can be fun and are especially useful if you have children as they sit below your sight-line in front of the television. However they are very informal and do become progressively more difficult to use as one ages, so don't expect your older visitors to

relish them. It is also worth pointing out that they do draw attention to the floor covering and its condition; also it is fairly isolating if the rest of the furniture is not at the same height. Low-level daybeds can work well with them, positioned both at the edge and in the centre of a room.

Left *Tato and Tatone are foam-filled floor stools upholstered in a nylon knit. Available in several shapes and colours, these pieces are actually quite supportive and firm to sit on making useful perches. Designed by Enrico Baleri and Denis Santachiara for Baleri Italia in 1995.*

Above *Sacco was designed by Piero Gatti, Cesare Paolini and Franco Teodoro in 1968-1969 for Zanotta. This anatomical easy chair is really an over-sized envelope containing polystyrene pellets. Often referred to as a 'sag bag', this versatile and extremely comfortable floor cushion forms to and supports your own natural shape – the ideal accompaniment to a Playstation.*

Left *Michael Marriott's Missed daybed, designed for SCP in 1997, is made from a beech frame with multi-density foam and stainless steel legs. Seemingly paying homage to Mies van der Rohe's seminal work, the final effect is refined for more straightforward manufacturing methods.*

side tables

Side tables and the ubiquitous 'coffee tables' are quite essential partners to the sofa, not only for displaying stylish art books and table lamps, but also for the more mundane mug of coffee and remote control for the television. Tables with some space for storage underneath can be very useful to give a tidy look to the room. Glass-topped tables are good for letting light through and giving a sense of space, as well as for setting on pattered rugs; do be careful if using glass or sharp-edged tables with young children around.

Above left *James Irvine's Fly Table, for Cappellini, 1995, has a coloured glass top on tubular metal framework. Available with many different glass colours shapes and sizes – chic and simple.*

Below *The Loop Table is made from plywood. Ample storage space under a low table surface makes this stylish piece particularly useful. Designed by Barber/Osgerby Associates for Cappellini in 1997.*

Above *Tris was designed by Antonio Citterio and Oliver Löw for Kartell, 1995-1996. The coloured plastic tops are set on plain metal legs. Clever and versatile, near identical nesting tables are useful in many different space-saving situations.*

storage & display

There are those things that you collect through life that you want to see around you, as much to reminisce as to decorate. Special and significant things from the past, art objects, perhaps gifts they often need to be displayed. And in a way that enhances a space rather than clutters it. There is also the need to store easily accessible things like books and CDs and various bits of equipment like telephones. Shelves and cabinets can be very useful here providing hidden and open access. Shelf units such as Jasper Morrison's *B.B. Bookcase* (shown opposite) can also function well as room dividers if you need to partition off a space.

Below Systemi *has a laquered timber carcass with a chromed steel under-structure. This immaculately finished piece is one of a systemised range of forbiddingly rectangular cupboards. Designed in 1996 by Piero Lissoni, manufactured by Cappellini.*

Opposite B.B. Bookcase *is made from laquered MDF and set on castors. Squaring the circle, this is good for storage, display and as a moveable room divider. Designed by Jasper Morrison in 1994, manufactured by Cappellini.*

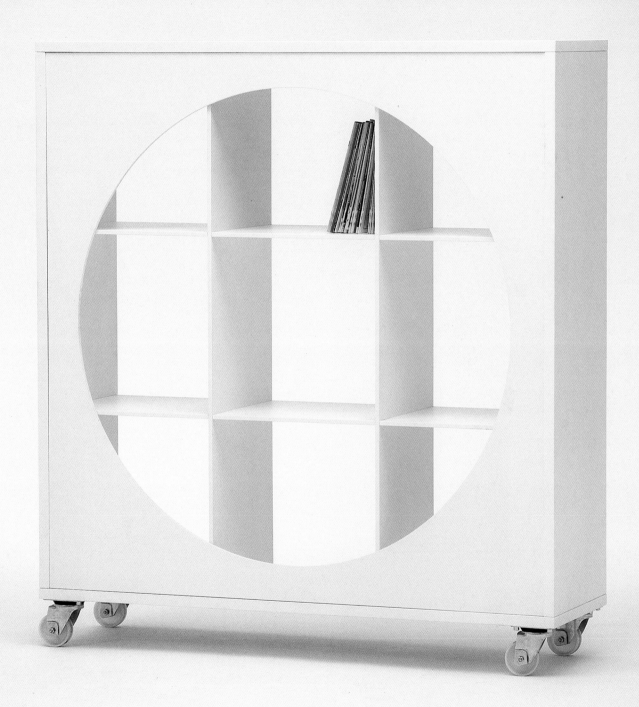

Below Blister Storage System *has a wood compositon body with metallic grey melamine finish and polypropylene doors in three colours. These are especially effective if used as multiples along a wall or as space dividers. Designed by Platt & Young in 1996 and manufactured by Driadé.*

Most shelves and cupboards are designed to fit against or fixed to the wall. Industrial designer Dieter Rams' seminal *606 Universal Shelving System* for Vitsoe designed is flexible, well thought out and still contemporary looking (pictured below). If you intend to fit a wall-mounted shelf-storage like this, make sure the wall is strong enough to take the weight, preferably fixing it to an exterior one. Shelves can look great when they are well ordered and not too untidy and designs with useful integrated closing cabinets work particularly well.

Tall cabinets with doors like the Platt & Young's *Blister Storage System* are a practical way of removing clutter from view – for that fashionable minimalist look the contoured front detail adds visual interest to an environment. However, they can become repositories for useless junk and they will also consume a lot of visual space in a small room. They provide particularly useful storage if you need the same room to function as a living room, home office or bedroom. Short sideboards are useful and easy to use especially in smaller rooms, the openness of its construction does not impact to badly on confined spaces.

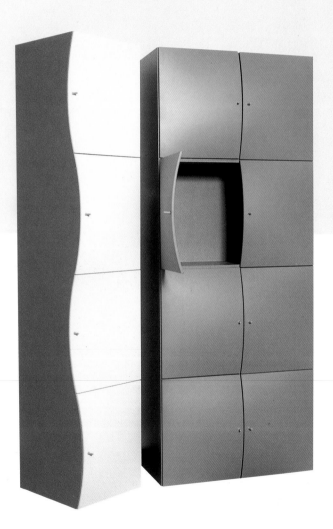

Right 606 Universal Shelving System *is an innovatively constructed system of shelves and storage. Designed in 1960 by Dieter Rams, the master of logical design; it still looks clean and fresh. Manufactured by Vitsoe.*

Above Matrjoska II Cabinet *has shaped layers of plywood with tubular steel legs. An interesting use of ply with the lamination grain emphasised as a principal part of the aesthetic. Designed by Olgoj Chorchoj in 1997.*

Left PAB System *is a well thought out and exquisitely engineered system of shelf and storage solutions. Designed by Studio Kairos in 1996 and manufactured by B&B Italia.*

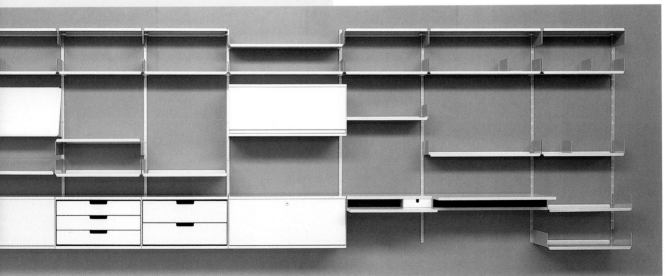

bedrooms

Bedrooms often are neglected as they are hidden from the view of visitors. They are, however, the room you spend most of your life in, all-be-it asleep. Not only do you need somewhere to store clothes and linen but also somewhere to dress and put discarded clothes. That spare dining chair or a simple bench (pictured below) is useful here, as is an arm-chair or lounger which would also perform this function well.

As for the bed… consider that you will be using this more than any other piece of furniture in your home, save perhaps a work chair. It is worth getting a really good mattress and as big a bed as is practical. The bed shown here, designed by Andrew Stafford, is particularly good as it has independent back supports which are useful for late-night reading.

Right Bedfordshire *has a maple moulded veneer, adjustable headboard, a solid maple frame with sprung beech slats and turned maple legs. Designed and manufactured by Andrew Stafford in 1998.*

Left *Alvar Aalto's* 153B Bench *is made from bent and solid birch. It is manufactured by Artek.*

Left *The Atlante wardrobe is made from satin finish aluminium with white or blue plate glass finish and frame edges in matt anodised aluminium. Designed by Studio Kairos in 1997 and manufactured by B&B Italia*

Below *The 90D stool/bedside table, designed by Alvar Aalto in 1930-33, is made from birch-faced plywood with a laminated top. Its compact design makes it ideal for the bedroom.*

There is an argument for the fewer clothes, the better – a wardrobe with a few favourite clothes in it is a joy to go to every morning, whereas a bulging mess makes a bad way to start the day. It is often a good strategy to be ruthless. Admittedly clothes are expensive but ask yourself: just how many pairs of tatty gardening shoes do I need? And tell me, how do you intend to get your waistline back to that halcyon size? An alternative option is to store out-of-season clothes in another room and change over as appropriate.

The elegant *Atlante* system (pictured opposite) is particularly ingenious and well thought-out. It provides a flexible interior storage combined with sliding doors for maximum space efficiency.

On a practical note, it is useful to have bedroom storage that incorporates different types and sizes of drawers, hanging rails and shelves. A dressing table is also worthwhile: the *Alice,* which includes a full-length mirror and stool, adds a stylish accent to any bedroom. Alternatively, a floor-standing cheval dressing mirror can also be a practical addition.

A wardrobe containing a few favourite clothes is a joy to use.

Right Alice *dressing table and stool, designed by Matthew Hilton in 1998, is manufactured by SCP. It has a steel frame with solid and veneered walnut drawer unit, a useful velvet-lined jewellery compartment and mirror.*

outdoors

Weather permitting it's great to be able to get out on a balcony, terrace or garden to enjoy the breeze and the sky, commune with nature, relax and entertain with some open-air cooking. Although there is no shortage of horrendous outdoor furniture (typified by garish floral vinyl cushions on white plastic) on the market, there are also some excellent pieces of well-considered contemporary furniture.

There are several designs available that work equally well indoors as out, Philippe Starck's *Lord Yo* chair is a practical and affordable option which also stacks and works extremely well around an indoor table. It has an elegant style, almost evocative of traditional wicker, combined with the practicality and durability of injection moulded polypropylene.

Sun loungers provide a relaxing way to enjoy the outdoors. Shin and Tomoko Azumi's shopping trolley technology chair and stool are simple and flexible; the stool works as a side table, and they stack well too.

Above Armframe, *Alberto Meda's 1996 design, has a polished cast-aluminium frame with nylon-mesh seating section. Elegant engineering chic at its most refined. Manufactured by Alias.*

Right *Richard Schultz' Leisure Collection Sun Lounger, designed in 1966 for B&B Italia, has a cast aluminium frame and woven mesh seat sections. One of the original modern garden furniture designs, still looking good after 30 years.*

multi-functional

furniture

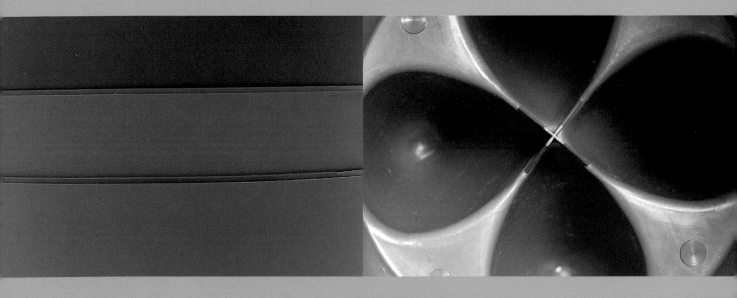

technology

Although we crave simplicity, technology can seem to have brought complexity rather than the promised quality of life. Modern lifestyles appear to becoming dominated by supposedly essential gadgetry upping the pace of our self-expectations. The problems posed by life's burgeoning plethora of imposing electronic equipment from video recorders and televisions to computers and printers and their attendant cabling are difficult to resolve with conventional desk furniture. These challenges are met in a variety of ways ranging from small moveable, customisable trolleys to fixed shelving systems like Dieter Rams' *606 Universal Shelving System* (see page 75) and the *Refolo* tech-trolleys shown here. These work well in many different ways depending on the equipment and usage required.

Konstantin Grcic's Refolo *trolley, designed for Driade in 1995, has a steel frame painted aluminium grey and sheet steel top in brick red. It is available in six function versions with colour-coded shelves for different uses, such as housing televisions, computers, stereos, etc. There are a variety of add-on functional accessories such as drawers and shelves which allow the trolleys to be used in other situations such as kitchen and bedrooms.*

sleeping

If you haven't got the luxury of a spare room, the occasional need to put someone up overnight or for a short stay or to occasionally sleep separately is often best addressed with a sofa-bed. These time-honoured, space-saving devices range from complex concertina mechanisms that fold out in an ingenious and improbable manner into double beds to the simple solutions requiring only fold-down armrests and the removal of cushions. Once poorly considered from a convenience point of view, the mechanisms have become so sophisticated, that they are now quite comfortable and user-friendly – sufficiently so to use this folding type on a regular daily sleeping basis. Some sofa-beds have space for bed linen and can be folded partially made-up. When they are folded they are difficult to distinguish from a regular sofa. This makes them ideal if you live in a single room studio flat.

The advantage of the simpler extending arm solution is that the fold-out leaves can often be used as perch seating to turn a stylish conventional sofa into a chaise-longue. This is particularly useful when you have many visitors to cater for and need to stretch your seating arrangements. they also tend to be more straightforward to use and in sofa mode more comfortable and less compromised than the concertina type. They are only generally acceptable as single beds and not as practical for everyday sleeping. Even if they are a little more expensive than a conventional sofa, they are probably a wise choice for the extra flexibility offered.

Jason was designed by Eoos Design for Walter Knoll. It has fabric upholstered seat cushions and body and removable back and side cushions; the legs are satin matt chromium-plated throughout. This is a good example of the modern approach to a convertible sofa.

versatile working

For people working from home, one of the most common issues is the need to double up the use of the dining table as a desk. The main challenge is the need to clear away and store the clutter of the day's work quickly, so that the untidy mess does not prey on your mind while relaxing. This can easily be achieved with a sideboard-style trolley which can be quickly wheeled out of sight.

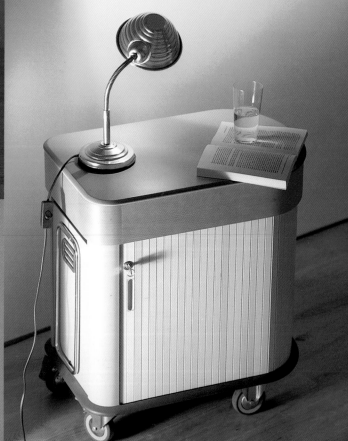

Pearson & Lloyd's Homer is a portable office. The side table trolley with shuttered sides, swivelling top surface and upper store space is made from a variety of materials including extruded aluminium, moulded plastic and formed ply. Manufactured by Knoll International in 1999.

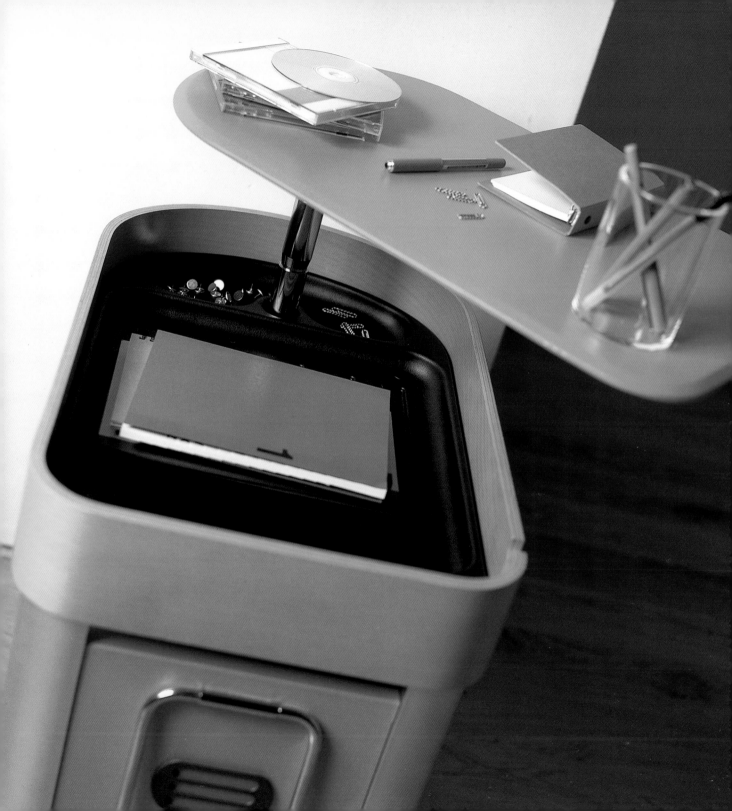

room effects

Buying furniture is the easy bit; choosing what is right for your home and arranging it to get the best out of it is where it gets complicated. It's comparatively easy to make a large space look good whereas a small space offers far greater challenges. The golden rule is to design the room for yourself and not for other peoples eyes. It is your home and you should feel comfortable in it.

The way you use furniture, lighting and colour will effect the apparent space of a room dramatically. As a general rule, using low furniture and lights will make a room look bigger; conversely the opposite is so.

The low table in this room acts centripedally, in almost a campfire way, drawing social interaction across it. The large picture window provides a spectacular city view and gives a wall-centric focus to the room. A large painting or an open fire would act in the same way.

Try not to arrange furniture right up against walls. Where possible, allow space so that light can spill behind and under pieces to give an airy effect. This is more easily achieved if you have upholstered furniture with legs.

Hard finishes and colours can be especially effective against a neutral setting with wall-to-wall-carpeted floor and plain walls providing uninterrupted lines to set off the sculptural, severe edges of the furniture. Carpet can also give a warmer, quieter ambience, contrasting with hard surfaces and accommodating the floor cushions well. Here the pale wood of the small stools and the wickerwork light help to introduce a more natural edge to the room.

Terence Woodgate's L-shaped sofa prescribes the main seating area well and is an eminently practical solution around the purpose-designed low coffee table which completes the visual square. It's important with this minimal look to give the individual pieces room to flourish and not to have too much clutter.

Harry Bertoia's seminal chromed wire weld-mesh *Diamond* chair appears almost transparent to light, causing no shadows and having very little visual impact on the space it occupies. Charles and Ray Eames' dining chairs with leather cushions produce a similar effect and complement the simple pedestal dining table they were designed to go with.

Tom Dixon's rotationally moulded *Jack* lights work well singly and in stacked multiples, giving a soft glow at night. By day they have a translucent luminescence when on and a solid sculptural presence when turned off. Lighting pale walls from a low level allows the light to reflect off the walls onto the ceiling and into the room, creating the effect of a high ceiling with soft shadows.

A fashionable flooring solution is the ubiquitous hard-wood strip. Used with rugs and soft furnishings, it gives a natural soft look. However, it does feel colder than carpet and reflects and transmits sound (particularly if you live in an apartment below it!). It's practical in that it doesn't stain in the way carpet does, which makes it a good choice in the kitchen or dining room, but be aware that it does mark easily if your furniture has sharp feet or missing foot ferrules and it can warp horribly if allowed to get wet.

Continuous flooring can link two adjoining rooms. Here kitchen and dining/living room merge seamlessly. The furniture has been carefully chosen for this effect – the hard-edged steel theme of the kitchen is continued in the choice of table, while the softer edged dining chairs link with the seating used at the far end of the room.

Big ideas can enhance the most unlikely of small spaces

White walls are effective at maximizing the available light and increasing the sense of space. Here the wide wooden shelf detailing softens the otherwise sterile effect that white can bring with it.

This ingenious small-scale mezzanine micro-workspace has been created in the space above a landing at the top of a flight of stairs. The translucent glass floor and staircase allow daylight to flood from windows above and below the platform. The neat, translucent white polyethylene *Chasm* chair, together with the small-scale wire-trussed workstation, enhances the overall sense of space and airiness. The directional spotlights playing on the bookcase combine with the work-light in the evening.

**The bedroom
is the one room
in the house
you can design
with purely yourself
in mind.**

You spend more time in the bedroom than any other room in the house so it is vitally important to get it right as it will colour your day ahead. When you wake up it is preferable to have a soft, calm environment to ease you gently into the day.

The pale wood of the furniture blends well with the blond hard wood floor of this compact bedroom, increasing the sense of space. Subdued walls, bed linen and window blinds continue the theme. Matthew Hilton's minimalist dressing and make-up table usefully combines a full height tilting mirror with drawers and a matching stool.

The reclining chair provides a secluded retreat for peaceful reading, as well as a useful spot for discarded clothes. A low-level bench placed at the foot of the bed also acts as short-term storage.

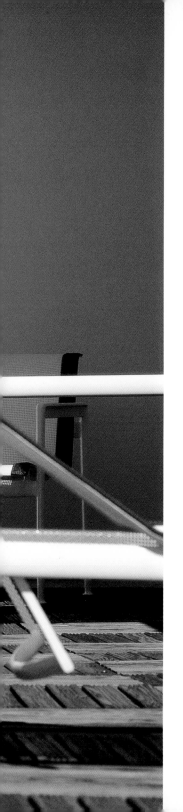

Out of doors bright sunlight can give harsh shadows which change with the weather, the seasons and time of day, colouring and softening the look of the garden, terrace or balcony.

Here the white ocean-liner style reclining lounge chairs together with the weathered hardwood duck boarding result in a distinctly nautical ambience. Panoramic glass windows and matching walls allow the inside of the apartment to blend almost seamlessly with the outside. This is also helped by the ceramic tiled floor which allows the same severe geometric furniture to be used inside and out, depending on the weather. This quiet, simple approach is a frequent trademark of early classic modernism.

contemporary

designers

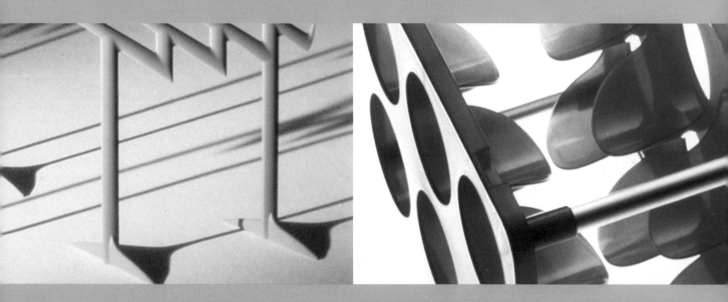

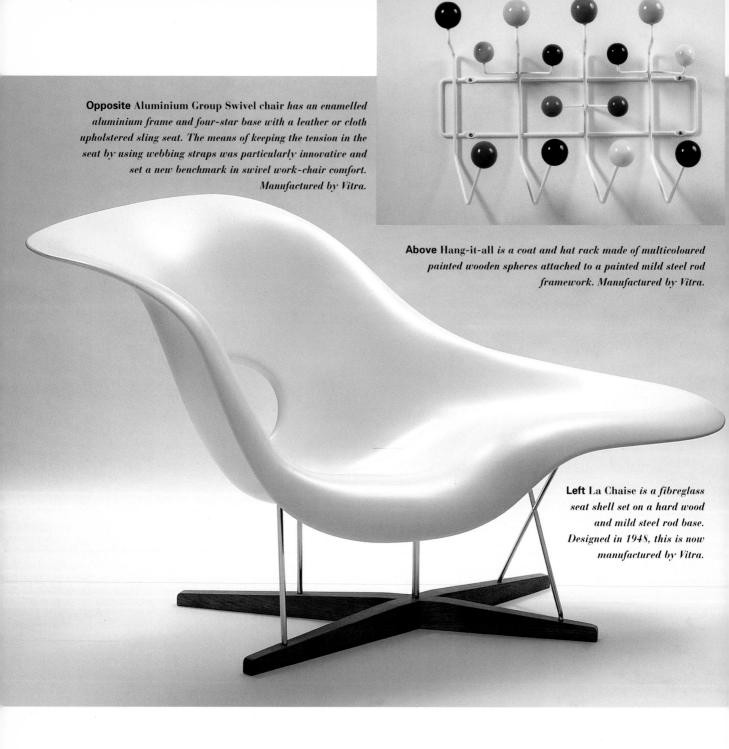

Opposite Aluminium Group Swivel chair *has an enamelled aluminium frame and four-star base with a leather or cloth upholstered sling seat. The means of keeping the tension in the seat by using webbing straps was particularly innovative and set a new benchmark in swivel work-chair comfort. Manufactured by Vitra.*

Above Hang-it-all *is a coat and hat rack made of multicoloured painted wooden spheres attached to a painted mild steel rod framework. Manufactured by Vitra.*

Left La Chaise *is a fibreglass seat shell set on a hard wood and mild steel rod base. Designed in 1948, this is now manufactured by Vitra.*

charles & ray eames

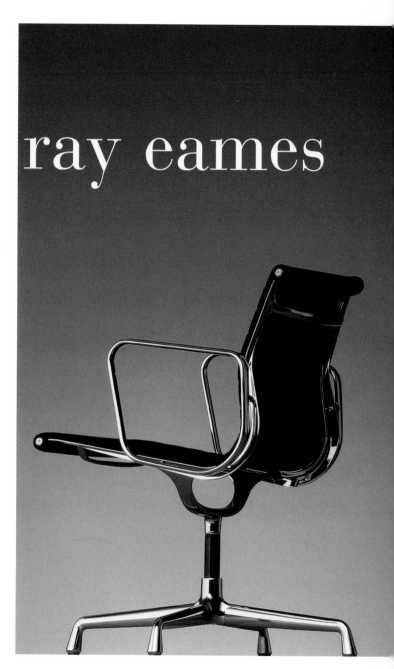

Charles Eames is considered one of the most important founders of 'modern' industrially produced furniture. He was born in 1907 and, with his wife Ray, formed a pioneering design partnership which was to have a profound influence on contemporary furniture worldwide.

They were chiefly famed for their innovative designs for Michigan furniture company Herman Miller. Based in California, they pioneered new technology and materials such as pressed steel, welded wire, fibreglass-reinforced plastics and moulded plywood. This led to innovative manufacturing processes as well as unusual organic forms. The Eames originally started exploring the use of moulded plywood with Eero Saarinen (see *Tulip* chair page 21). Fibreglass-reinforced plastic had only been used in aircraft production until the Eames came across it in a war surplus store. This new material suited the organic forms they were working on. Although Charles died in 1978, many of his designs continue to be popular and are still in production.

antonio citterio

Graduating as an architect in Milan, Citterio started his design practice 1972 and was joined by senior partner Terry Dwan from 1987-95. They have worked on a large number of mainly commercial environmental projects, designing factories, offices and shops throughout the Europe, USA and Japan.

Significantly Citterio has always worked prolifically as an industrial design consultant too and has also designed furniture for many notable manufacturers including B&B Italia, Flos, Kartell and Vitra (for whom he also designed showrooms and a factory). Although not a natural self-publicist he has quietly had a truly prodigious output and is probably chiefly known for his soft furnishings and influential office furniture.

He has a marked reputation for being able to produce highly marketable, commercial designs. His work is usually technically innovative and is generally exemplified by its ingenuity, functional efficiency, quiet elegance and superb attention to detail.

Left *The stackable* **Minni Chair** *has an injection-moulded plastics back and seat with legs and arms in solid beech-wood. Manufactured by Halifax.*

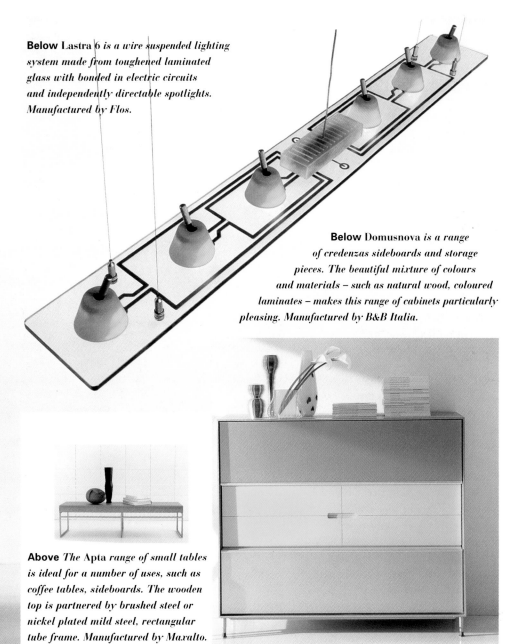

Below Lastra 6 *is a wire suspended lighting system made from toughened laminated glass with bonded in electric circuits and independently directable spotlights. Manufactured by Flos.*

Below Domusnova *is a range of credenzas sideboards and storage pieces. The beautiful mixture of colours and materials – such as natural wood, coloured laminates – makes this range of cabinets particularly pleasing. Manufactured by B&B Italia.*

Below Charles *is an extremely comfortable and well-made flexible sofa system. The excellent proportions and refined looks allow this to work well in a variety of situations. Manufactured by B&B Italia.*

Above *The* Apta *range of small tables is ideal for a number of uses, such as coffee tables, sideboards. The wooden top is partnered by brushed steel or nickel plated mild steel, rectangular tube frame. Manufactured by Maxalto.*

philippe starck

Mad-Genius-Showman is probably the best way to describe the prolific French designer Philippe Starck – he is a living phenomenon. Predictably unpredictable, he works in all fields of design including interiors, furniture, domestic artefacts, lighting and graphics – he has even designed motorcycles. Originally an architect, he is best known for the charismatic forms of his products.

Without constraint he seems to have single-handedly created an international design style which combines strong conceptual ideas, functional ingenuity, wit and provocative form with astonishing attention to detail. Not only does he look for innovative design solutions, he also combines this with an exploration of materials and process technology. The boldness of his irreverent approach together with his sheer volume of work has made him perhaps today's best known and most noticed furniture designer.

The originality and lack of compromise in his work sometimes meant that it did not gain immediate public acceptance. However, his influence on all areas of the design industry and contemporary design is difficult to refute. Perhaps he could be better described as a sort of court jester with his ability to imaginatively address real design issues in a charmingly light-hearted manner.

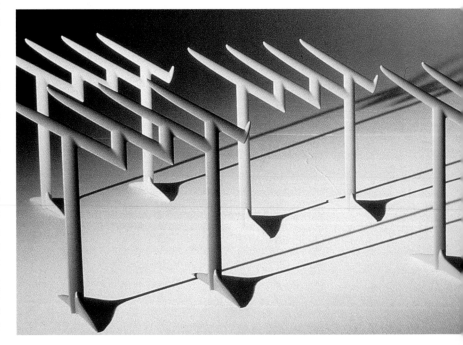

Below left Claudia Evangelista *is an injection-moulded plastic magazine rack. Innovatively the magazines are hung with their spines open over the plastic blades. Manufactured by Kartell.*

Right Romeo Moon *is a cast fluted glass suspended from three steel wires. Manufactured by Flos, it is also available in fabric, in two sizes and in matching floor and table versions.*

Below Le Marie *is a clear and colourless polycarbonate moulded seat shell with integral polycarbonate legs. Manufactured by Kartell.*

Dr No *comprises a plastic moulded seat shell with painted metal legs. Available in a range of ice cream colours, these stacking chairs work well inside and out and are surprisingly comfortable – compare to the* Lord Yo *chairs on page 80. Manufactured by Kartell.*

jasper morrison

Known for the extreme clarity of his design solutions, Morrison has a serene ability to distil his works down with uncomplicated elegant design solutions. Quiet and unassuming – quite the opposite of Philippe Starck – he actually studied Furniture Design at London's Royal College of Art. He quickly made his mark with early pieces such as *The Thinking Man's Chair* (see page 30) which established his cerebral approach to tackling design challenges.

In addition to his furniture designs, he has worked at an international level on a wide variety of design projects including urban transport systems, architectural fittings, household goods and tableware. All his work bears the hallmark of severe sophisticated simplicity and an almost 'Germanic Puritanism'. His work typifies Mies Van der Rohe's dictum 'less is more'. He is most definitely the designer's designer.

Right Lima Chair *is constructed from plastic moulded seat slats on tubular metal frame. Manufactured by Cappellini.*

Right Bottle Rack, *designed for Magis, is made from injection-moulded polypropylene with anodised aluminium connecting tubular sub-structure. A very simple idea using common components, this has been copied by many others but never bettered.*

The nice thing about these Glo-Ball lights is that they are not completely spherical but are slightly squashed, like a tangerine. This point was emphasized in their advertising campaign. Manufactured by Flos.

Above *The refined looking organic aluminium forgings of the Lever Handle 1144 fit snugly into the palm. Actually designed for the contract market, this is nonetheless just as suitable for domestic applications. Manufactured by FSB.*

factfile tips on buying furniture

✳ Make sure that whatever you buy will fit through the front door and through all access routes to its resting point.

✳ Always test furniture for comfort, not just its looks.

✳ Make sure that a table can seat as many as you require.

✳ Check that the ticket price includes delivery and any taxes such as VAT.

✳ Check upholstery materials comply with fire regulations.

✳ Ask if customer's own material (COM) is an option.

✳ If the product is to be used outside, check if it is made of suitable materials.

✳ Carefully check the item on delivery for faults and damage before accepting it.

✳ Remember that some furniture can take 8-10 weeks to arrive.

stockists & designers

The following stores stock a good range of contemporary furniture. If you are looking for a particular piece, it is worth telephoning the store first to check they still carry the range.

ABC TRADING
(Furniture Gallery)
15–17 Church Road
Hendon
London NW4 4EB
Tel: 020 8202 0525

ARAM DESIGNS
5–7 Kean Street
London WC2B 4AT
Tel: 020 7240 3933

ARIA
295 Upper Street
London N1 2TU
Tel: 020 7704 1999
*Range includes furniture by
Phillippe Starck, Verner Panton,
Stefano Giovannoni, Nigel
Coates, Ron Arad*

ATKINSON CONTRACTS
1 Abbeygate
Leicester LE4 OAA
Tel: 0116 262 9494
*Range includes furniture by
Vitra, Herman Miller, Cassina,
Flos, Arteluce, Artemide*

ATOMIC
Plumptre Square
Nottingham NG1 1JF
Tel: 0115 941 5577
*Range includes furniture by
Simon Siegel, Kartell, Philippe
Starck, Eames, Vitra, Le
Corbusier Classics, Noguchi*

ATRIUM LTD
Centrepoint
22-24 St Giles High Street
London WC2H 8TA
Tel: 020 7379 7288
*Range includes furniture by
Cattelan, Interlubke, Moroso,
Enea, Fritz Hansen*

BATIK INTERIORS
60B Bedford Street
Belfast BT2 7FH
Tel: 01232 249311
*Range includes furniture by
Doug Elliott MD, Zanotta, Enzo
Mari, Castiglioni,
Le Corbusier, Zanuso*

BEDFORDSHIRE
95 Redchurch Street
London E2 7DS
Tel: 020 7613 0054
Design consultants

BISLEY OFFICE FURNITURE
Northumberland House
155-157 Great Portland Street
London W1W 6QP
Tel: 020 7436 7111

**BOND PROJECTS UK
LTD**
Prism Design Studio
38 Grosvenor Gardens
London SW1W OEB
Tel: 020 7730 3011

CAZ SYSTEMS
17–19 Church Street
Brighton BN1 1RB
Tel: 01273 326471
*Range includes furniture by
Philippe Starck, Magistretti,
Eileen Grey, Sottsass*

*Secondhand shops (see page
124) are also a good source of
contemporary furniture.
George Nelson's seminal chair,
whose organic form has been
influential in recent times, was
originally made by Knoll.*

CENTRAL
33-35 Little Clarendon Street
Oxford OX1 2HU
Tel: 01865 311141
Range includes furniture by
Tekno, Magis, Ligne Roset,
Philippe Starck, Matthew Hilton

CHAPLINS
477-507 Uxbridge Road
Hatch End, Pinner
Middlesex HA5 4JF
Tel: 020 8421 1779
Range includes furniture by
Giorgetti, Porada, Ligne Roset,
Interlubke, De Sede, Fendi

CO-EXISTENCE
288 Upper Street
London N1 2TZ
Tel: 020 7354 8817
Range includes furniture by
B&B Italia, Alias, Walter Knoll,
Kartell, Artek, Vitra, Lammhults

CONRAN COLLECTION
12 Conduit Street
London W1S 2XQ
Tel: 020 7399 0710

CONRAN SHOP
Michelin House
81 Fulham Road
London SW3 6RD
Tel: 020 7589 7401
and
55 Marylebone High Street
London W1M 3AE
Tel: 020 7723 2223

CONRAN & PARTNERS
22 Shad Thames
London SE1 2YU
Tel: 020 7403 8899
Design consultants

DAVID VILLAGE INTERIORS
c/o Illume
285 Ecclesall Road
Sheffield S11 8NX
Tel: 0114 2634260
Range includes furniture
by Kartell

DESIGN CONSCIOUS
www.design-conscious.co.uk
Range includes furniture by
Philippe Starck, Ron Arad,
Stefano Giovanonni, Vico
Magistretti

DESIGN SHOP
10 Richmond Hill
Richmond
Surrey TW10 6QX
Tel: 020 8241 2421
Range includes furniture by
Ryan & Co, Kartell, Philippe
Starck, Wireworks

DOMAIN
2 High Seat Copse
High Street
Billingshurst
West Sussex RH14 9SN
Tel: 01403 257201
Range includes furniture by
B&B Italia, Bonacina, Maxalto,
Rolf Benz, Tonelli

EQUIPOISE LIGHTING
107 Nottingham Road
Derby DE1 3QR
Tel: 01332 360 370
Range includes furniture by
Kartell, Flos

FRITZ HANSEN
20-22 Rosebury Avenue
London EC1R 4UA
Tel: 020 7837 2030

FUNCTION
Unit 18
1b Darnley Road
London E9 6QH
Tel: 020 8525 5353

GEOFFREY DRAYTON
104 High Street
Epping
Essex CM16 4AF
Tel: 01992 573929
and
85 Hampstead Road
London NW1 2PL
Tel: 020 7387 5840
Range includes furniture by
Cassina, B&B Italia,
Interlubke

GRAHAM & GREEN
4, 7 & 10 Elgin Crescent
London W11 2JA
Tel: 020 7727 4594

HABITAT
Tel: 0845 60 10 740
For nearest store

HAUS
The Green Building
3-4 Crow Street
Templebar
Dublin 2
Tel: 0035 31 6795155
Range includes furniture by
Zanotta, Cassina, Flos,
B&B Italia

HAUS
23-25 Mortimer Street
London W1N 7RJ
Tel: 020 7255 2557
Range includes furniture by
Knoll, Vitra, B&B Italia, Fiam,
Techno

HEAL & SON LTD
196 Tottenham Court Road
London W1P 9LD
Tel: 020 7636 1666
and
234 Kings Road
London SW3
Tel: 020 7349 8411

and
49–51 Eden Street
Kingston-Upon-Thames
Surrey KT1 1BW
Tel: 020 8614 5900
and
Tunsgate
Guildford
Surrey GU1 3QU
Tel: 01483 796500

HERMAN MILLER
Maple House
Tottenham Court Road
London W1P 9LL
Tel: 020 7388 7331

HILLE INTERNATIONAL
Cross Street
Darwen
Lancashire BB3 2PW
Tel: 01254 778850
and
Business Design Centre
52 Upper Street
London N1 0QH
Tel: 020 7288 6202

IKEA
Tel: 020 8208 5600
for nearest store

INFLATE
28 Exmouth Market
London EC1R 4QE
Tel: 020 7251 5453

JANE ATFIELD
244 Grays Inn Road
London WC1X 8JR
Tel: 020 7833 0018

KNOLL INTERNATIONAL
East Market Building
London Central Markets
London EC1A 9PQ
Tel: 020 7236 6656

INHOUSE
24-26 Wilson Street
Glasgow G1 1SS
Tel: 0141 5523322
and
28 Howe Street
Edinburgh EH3 6TG
Tel: 0131 225 2888
*Range includes furniture by
Driade, Cassina, Molteni, Flos,
Artemide, Alessi, Reidel*

MASKREY'S LTD
62-64 White Lady Road
Clifton
Bristol BS8 2QA
Tel: 0117 9738401
and
116-120 Whitchurch Road
Cardiff CF14 3YL
Tel: 029 2022 9371

MUJI
Tel: 020 7323 228
for nearest store

NEW ROOMS
51 High Street
Cheltenham
Gloucester GL50 1DX
Tel: 01242 237977
*Range includes furniture by
Aero, Kartell*

**NOEL HENNESSY
FURNITURE**
6 Cavendish Square
London W1G 0PD
Tel: 020 7323 3360

NICEHOUSE
The Italian Centre Courtyard
Ingram Street
Glasgow G1 1DN
Tel: 0141 553 1377
*Range includes furniture by
BRS, Cappellini, Montis, Parri,
Le Corbusier, One Foot Taller*

ORA GALLERY
239 Sharrovale Road
Sheffield S11 8ZE
Tel: 0114 2661444
*Range includes furniture by
Alessi, Kartell, Magis*

PURVES & PURVES
220–224 Tottenham Court Road
London W1T 7QE
Tel: 020 7580 8223
*Range includes furniture by
B&B Italia, Kartell, Riva, Hitch
Mylins, Herman Miller*

**PURVES & PURVES
ACCESSORIES**
Canada Place
Canary Wharf
London E14 5AH
Tel: 020 7719 1169

**RALPH CAPPER
INTERIORS**
10a Little Peter Street
Manchester M16 4PS
Tel: 0161 236 6929
*Range includes furniture by
Cassina - Le Corbusier, Lloyd
Wright, Starck, Magistrelli,
Bellini, Mackintosh; Fritz Hansen
Jacobsen, Magistretti,
Magnussen Kjaerholm; Vitra -
Eames, Bellini, Citterio; Driade -
Starck, Lusca, Lovegrove*

RUTH ARAM SHOP
65 Heath Street
Hampstead
London NW3 6UG
Tel: 020 7431 4008
*Range includes furniture by
Kartell, Magis, Albed, Fritz
Hansen, LSA International,
Glascoch, Rexite, Flos*

SAME
146 Brick Lane
London E1 6RV
Tel: 020 7247 9992
*Range includes furniture by
Asplund, David Design,
Eurolounge, DMD, Ingo Maurer,
Box Design*

SCP
135-139 Curtain Road
London EC2A 3BX
Tel: 020 7739 1869
*Range includes furniture by
Matthew Hilton, Terence
Woodgate, Michael Marriott,
Andrew Stafford, Jasper
Morrison, Le Corbusier*

SET
100 High Street
Leicester LE1 5YP
Tel: 0116 251 0161
*Range includes furniture by
Philippe Starck, Magis, Kartell,
Race Furniture*

SPACE
214 Westbourne Grove
London W11 2RH
Tel: 020 7727 0134
*Range includes furniture by Edra,
Michael Young, Michael Sodeau,
Cec Le Page and their own range
of leather and sheepskin floor
cushions, beanbags*

STEPHEN NEALL
Prince Albert Row
79 Station Parade
Harrogate
North Yorkshire HG1 1ST
Tel: 01423 521288

THE HOME
Salts Mill
Victoria Road
Saltaire
Bradford BD18 3LB
Tel: 01274 530 770
*Range includes furniture by
Bernini - Achille Castiglioni/Joe
Colombo, Warren Macarthur -
Classicon, Progetti*

VIADUCT FURNITURE LTD
1-10 Summers Street
London EC1R 5BD
Tel: 020 7278 8456
*Range includes furniture by
Driade, Montis, MDF Italia,
Pallucco Italia, Zeus*

VITSOE
85 Arlington Avenue
London N1 7BA
Tel: 020 7354 8444

WEDROC TRADING COMPANY
41b Smith Street
Warwick CV34 4JA
Tel: 01926 492161

WIREWORKS
131a Broadley Street
London NW8 8BA
Tel: 020 7724 8856

28 LIGHTING
28 East Street
Saffron Walden
Essex CB10 1AR
Tel: 01799 522133
*Range includes furniture by
Porro, Fontana Arte, Perobell,
Divani Living, Kartell, Zanotta,
ICF, Danerka*

Original and secondhand furniture

ATOMIC
Plumptre Square
Nottingham NG1 1JF
Tel: 0115 941 5577

CENTURY DESIGN
68 Marylebone High Street
London W1M 3AQ
Tel: 020 7487 5100

DAVID GILL
60 Fulham Road
London SW3 6HH
Tel: 020 7589 5946

GALLERY 25
6 Halkin Arcade
West Halkin Street
London SW1X 8JT
Tel: 020 7235 5178

PLACES & SPACES
30 Old Town
London SW4 0LB
Tel: 020 7498 0998

RETRO HOME
20, 32 and 34 Pembridge Road
London W11 3HN
Tel: 020 7221 2055

THE STABLES
Camden Market
Chalk Farm Road
London NW1 8AH
Tel: 020 7485 5511

SUCCESSION
179 Westbourne Grove
London W11 2SB
Tel: 020 7727 0580

THEMES & VARIATIONS
231 Westbourne Grove
London W11 2SE
Tel: 020 7727 5531

TOM TOM
42 New Compton Street
London WC2H 8DA
Tel: 020 7240 7909

TWENTY TWENTY ONE
274 Upper Street
London N1 2UA
Tel: 020 7288 1996

Commissioning furniture

CRAFTS COUNCIL
44a Pentonville Road
Islington
London N1 9BY
Tel: 020 7278 7700
For commissioning crafts-based designers and one-offs.

Auction houses

These auction houses all now hold twentieth century design sales.

BONHAMS
Montpelier Street
London SW7 IHH
Tel: 020 7393 3900
and
65-69 Lots Road
London SW10 ORN
Tel: 020 7351 7111

CHRISTIE'S
8 Kings Street
London SW1Y 6QT
Tel: 020 7839 9060
and
85 Old Brompton Road
London SW7 3LD
Tel: 020 7581 7611

SOTHEBY'S
34-35 New Bond Street
London W1A 2AA
Tel: 020 7293 5000

Places to visit

CRAFTS COUNCIL
44a Pentonville Road
London N1 9BY
Tel: 020 7278 770

DESIGN MUSEUM
Butlers Wharf
28 Shad Thames
London SE1 2YD
Tel: 020 7403 6933

GEFFRYE MUSEUM
Kingsland Road
London E2 8EA
Tel: 020 7739 9893

GLASGOW SCHOOL OF ART
167 Renfrew Street
Glasgow
Tel: 0141 353 4500

HILLHEAD HOUSE/ HUNTERIAN ART GALLERY
University of Glasgow
Hillhead Street
Glasgow
Tel: 0141 330 5431

THE SCIENCE MUSEUM
Exhibition Road
London SW7 2DD
Tel: 020 7938 8000

THE TWENTIETH CENTURY GALLERY
Victoria & Albert Museum
Cromwell Road
London SW7 2RL
Tel: 020 7938 8500

Further reading

The following books provide more detailed information on contemporary design and furniture and the individual designers mentioned in this book.

Thomas Hauffe: *Design: A Concise History*
Lawrence King, 1998,
ISBN 1 856-69134 9

The Work of Charles and Ray Eames - A Legacy of Invention
Vitra Design Museum
Abrams, ISBN 0 8109 1799 8

Francois Baudot: *Eileen Gray*
Thames Hudson, 1998,
ISBN 0500 018533 7

Tom Dixon
Architecture, Design and Technology Press, 1990,
ISBN 18 5454 8425

Jasper Morrison - Designs, Projects and Drawings 1981-1989
Architecture, Design and Technology Press, 1990,
ISBN 1 85454 4357

Starck
Benedikt Taschen Verlag GmbH,
ISBN 3 8228 8500 2

100 Masterpieces From The Vitra Design Museum
1996, ISBN 3 9804070 3 9

Penny Sparke: *Furniture – Twentieth Century Design*
E.P. Ditton, 1986,
ISBN 0 525 24413 1

Leslie Pina: *Fifties Furniture*
Schiffer, 1996,
ISBN 07643 0152 7

Leslie Pina: *Furniture 2000 - Modern Classics and New Designs in Production*
Schiffer, 1998,
ISBN 0 7643 0496 8

Ugo La Pietra: *Gio Ponti*
Rizzoli, 1988, ISBN 0 8478 1950 7

Alan Crawford: *Charles Rennie Mackintosh*
Thames & Hudson,
ISBN 0 500 20283 4

Charlotte & Peter Fiell:
Modern Chairs
Benedikt Taschen Verlag GmbH,
1993, ISBN 3 8228 9451 6

Charlotte & Peter Fiell:
1000 Chairs
Benedikt Taschen Verlag GmbH,
1997, ISBN 3 8228 7965 7

397 Chairs
Abrams, 1988,
ISBN 0 8109 1698 3

Mel Byars: *50 Chairs – Innovations in Design and Materials*
Rotovision, 1997,
ISBN 2 88046 49

Mel Byars: *50 Tables – Innovations in Design and Materials*
Rotovision, 1997,
ISBN 2 88046 311 4

Peta Levi:
New British Design 1998
Mitchell Beazley, 1998,
ISBN 1 84000 099 6

Thomas Hauffe:
Design – A Concise History
Laurence King, 1998,
ISBN 1 85669 134 4

Edward Lucie-Smith: *Furniture – A Concise History*
Thames & Hudson, 1997,
ISBN 0 500 20172 2

Pocket Design Directory
Janvier Publishing, 1998,
ISBN 0 95184 949 2

Phillippe Garner: *Sixties Design*
Benedikt Taschen Verlag GmbH,
ISBN 3 8228 8934 2

Alexander von Vegesack: *Thonet*
Hazar, 1996, ISBN 1 874371 26 1

Lynn Gordon: *ABC of Design*
Chronicle Books, 1996,
ISBN 0 8118 1141 7

George H. Marcus: *Design in the Fifties When Everyone Went Modern*
Prestel, ISBN 3 7913 1939 6

Vico Magistretti's **Flower Chair** *is similar in shape to* **Incisa** *on page 11. This petite piece is made in a manufacturing-friendly manner without losing its sophistication. Manufactured by De Padova.*

index

First published in Great Britain in 1999 by
Conran Octopus Ltd
a part of Octopus Publishing Group
2–4 Heron Quays, London E14 4JP
www.conran-octopus.co.uk

This paperback edition published in 2003

ISBN 1 84091 315 0

Commissioning Editor Denny Hemming
Series Editor Gillian Haslam
Managing Editor Kate Bell
Index Vicky Robinson

Creative Director Leslie Harrington
Art Editor Lucy Gowans
Stylist Emma Thomas
Production Zoe Fawcett

British Library Cataloguing-in-Publication Data.
A catalogue record for this book is available from the
British Library.

Colour origination by Sang Choy International, Singapore

Printed in China

Acknowledgments

Special thanks to Tim Gadd for research and for all his help behind the
scenes. Thanks, also, to Kathryn Mills and Helen Thompson.

The authors and publishers wish to thank the following for their
considerable help and assistance: Alexis Nishihata at **Aero**; Linda
Gledstone at **Atrium**; Edward Barber and Jason Osgerby at **Barber
Osgerby Associates**; Andrew Stafford at **Bedfordshire**; Marcus Stevens
at **Bisley**; Gill Hicks at **Blueprint**; Clemente Cavigioli at **Cavigioli**;
Annabel Buckingham and Nick Cooney at **Coexistence**; Jamie Abbot at
Conran Holdings; Abigail Bond, James Peto and Eric Kentley at **Design
Museum**; Elena Graves at **Eurolounge**; Nicholas Howard; Peter Lewis at
Function; Jonathon Sherwood at **Haus**; Colin Shergold at **Herman
Miller**; Lindsey Nicolson at **Hille International**; Jane Atfield at **Kiosk**;
Sarah Cottan at **Knoll International**; Vallery McInnes at **McInnes Cook**;
Andrew Harrold and Sara Jones at **Nicehouse**; Luke Pearson and Tom
Lloyd at **Pearson Lloyd**; Joanne Leyland at **Purves & Purves**; Piers
Roberts and Fiona Dodd at **Same**; Sheridan Coakley at **SCP**; Simon
Alderson at **Twenty Twenty One**; James Mair and Tamara Caspersz at
Viaduct; Natalie Keuroghlian at **Vitra**; Mark Adams at **Vitsoe**; Anna
Burnett at **Wireworks**.

We would also like to thank the following people for allowing us to
photograph their homes and premises: Ou Baholyodhin, Sharon
Bowles of Bowles & Linares, Joe Hagan, Mei Teck Wong and Juan Dols
of Dols Wong Architects.

With thanks to the following for the kind loan of transparencies:
Andrew Stafford (p.76-77 photo Tariq Dajani), **B&B Italia** (p.80 bottom
and p.115 *Apta* table), **Atrium** (p.34 *21 Hotel Grand Suite* chair),
Cappellini (p.59 *Juli*), **Cassina** (p.9 *Wink* chair photo Andrea Zani),
Coexistence (p.90-91 *Jason* sofa and p.115 *Domusnova*), **The Conran
Collection** (p.46 *Arion* bar stool and p.70-71 *Loop* table), **De Padova**
(p.11 *Incisa* chair and p.125 *Flower* chair photo Luciano Soave), **Driade**
(p.88-89 *Refolo* trolley photo Emilio Tremolado), **Flos** (p.115 *Lastra*
light), **Lucy Pope** (p.50 *Powwow table*), **Jasper Morrison** (p.118-119),
Ron Arad (p.55 *Fantastic Plastic Elastic* chair), **Studio Citterio** (p.114
portrait of Antonio Citterio by Gitty Darugar), **Twenty Twenty One**
(p.121 *George Nelson* chair), **Viaduct** (p.39 *King Tubby*, p.46 *Cheap Chic*
bar stool, p.52 *Camelion* chair, p.65 *Olivier* chair), **Vitra** (p.24 *Wiggle*
chair, p.28 Eames chair, p.31 *How High The Moon*, p.36 Eames *Lounge
Chair and Ottoman*, p.54 *Ply* chair, *LCW* chair and *Panton* chair, p.59
Meda chair, p.64 *Coconut* chair, p.112-113 coat rack and portrait of
Charles and Ray Eames), **Vitsoe** (p.75 *606* Universal shelving system).

Thanks to the following companies for the loan of additional furniture
and acessores for photography: **LSA International** (01932 789721),
Purves & Purves (020 7580 8223), **Aero** (020 7351 0511), **Same**
(020 7247 9992), **Alma Home** (020 7377 0762), **Egg** (020 7235 9315),
Space (020 7229 6533), **Maxfield Parrish** (020 7252 5225), **Habitat**
(0645 334433), **Eurolounge** (020 7792 5477).